HOW TO
BE THE PARENT
*you always
wanted to be*

HOW TO BE THE PARENT
you always wanted to be

Adele Faber
and
Elaine Mazlish

Illustrations by
Kimberly Ann Coe

HYPERION

New York

The International Center for Creative Thinking
Mamaroneck, New York

CONTENTS

Dear Friends,

Now that you have your personal parenting workshop kit, you're probably wondering what to do first. We recommend that you start by playing both of the *How To Be the Parent You Always Wanted To Be* audio tapes. After listening to them, you might think to yourself, "I like what I heard, but I don't know if I could ever do it." Since it took us a long time to learn the skills we now teach, that reaction doesn't surprise us. It's natural to find yourself repeating to your children the very things your parents said to you—both positive and negative. And it's natural to wonder if it's possible to change any deeply ingrained negative patterns.

That's the reason for this workbook—to give you a chance to practice this new way of communicating so that it becomes an easy and comfortable part of the way you express yourself. The bonus for all your hard work is that your children won't have too much to unlearn when they become parents. (And you won't have too much to criticize when you become a grandparent.)

We hope you enjoy looking at the cartoons and doing the exercises. We feel confident that your children will enjoy the new sounds in the house.

Warmest wishes,

Adele Faber
Elaine Mazlish

Adele Faber
Elaine Mazlish

PART
I

PRINCIPLES
and skills

ABOUT *feelings*

"What bothers me about
kids is how they cry and
carry on over the least
little thing. And there's
no reasoning with them."

ABOUT FEELINGS

When their unhappy feelings are denied or dismissed, children often become more upset.

Even a logical solution from the parent doesn't seem to help.

CHILDREN WANT YOU TO KNOW WHAT THEY'RE FEELING

Sometimes it helps if you just listen.

Sometimes a word, like "oh" or "mmm," lets them know you understand.

Sometimes it helps if you can name the feeling.

I tried to glue it back on but it kept falling off.

That must have been frustrating!

Most children appreciate it when you give them in fantasy what they can't have in reality.

I bet you wish you could say, "Abracadabra", and your rabbit would grow a whole new ear.

You can accept children's feelings even when you decide to limit their actions.

PRACTICE
acknowledging feelings

Part I

In each of the following examples, choose the response that shows you understand.

1 Child: Daddy nearly killed me when he took that splinter out of my finger.

Parent: **a** It couldn't have been that bad.

b Sounds as if it really hurt.

c He did it for your own good.

2 Child: Just because of a little snow, the coach canceled our big game.

Parent: **a** That must be a disappointment. You were all "psyched" to play and now you have to wait.

b Don't let it get you down. You'll have plenty of other chances to play.

c Your coach made the right decision. Sometimes a little snow can turn into a big snow.

3 A child is playing with your new string of beads.

Parent: **a** How many times have I told you never to touch my jewelry? You're a bad girl.

b Please don't play with Mommy's beads. You'll break them.

c You really like my new beads. The trouble is they break easily. You can play with these wooden beads or with this scarf.

4 **Child:** I don't like spiders.

    Parent: **a** Oh.

            b Why not? They're part of nature.

            c I don't like them either.

5 **Child:** (looking anxious) I have to take my math final tomorrow.

    Parent: **a** Relax. I'm sure you'll do well.

            b If you had spent more time studying, you wouldn't be worried now.

            c You sound worried. I'll bet you wish it were over and done with.

6 Your child is eating spaghetti with his/her fingers.

    Parent: **a** Your table manners are disgusting.

            b I know it's easier to eat spaghetti with your fingers. When the family eats together, we'd like you to use a fork.

            c I can't believe that at your age you're still eating with your fingers.

7 **Child:** David wants to take me to the school dance. He's really nice, but I don't know . . .

    Parent: **a** Oh go. You'll see, you'll have fun.

            b Well make up your mind. Either you want to go or you don't.

            c So part of you wants to go and part of you isn't sure.

8 **Child:** I'm gonna run away from home.
Parent: **a** Fine, I'll help you pack.
b You're being silly. I don't want to hear that kind of talk.
c You sound very unhappy. I'll bet you wish a lot of things were different around here.

Answers: 1b, 2a, 3c, 4a, 5c, 6b, 7c, 8c

PRACTICE
acknowledging feelings

Part II

Under each of the following statements, write:

a an unhelpful response
b a helpful response that acknowledges feelings

1 "I'm never going to play with Susie again!"

Unhelpful: _____

_____

_____

_____

Helpful: _____

_____

_____

_____

2 "How come my sister gets so many birthday presents?"

Unhelpful: _____

_____

_____

_____

Helpful: _____

_____

_____

_____

3 "This picture I made is ugly."

Unhelpful: _____

_____

_____

_____

Helpful: _____

_____

_____

_____

4 "My teacher gives us too many tests."

Unhelpful: _____

_____

_____

_____

Helpful: _____

_____

_____

_____

5 A child looks unhappy.

Unhelpful: _____

_____

_____

_____

Helpful: _____

_____

_____

☰ POSSIBLE ANSWERS ☰

Here are some responses to the child's statements on the previous page. There is no such thing as one "correct" answer. As long as we acknowledge a child's feelings with respect, we are helpful.

1 "I'm never going to play with Susie again!"

    Unhelpful: You don't really mean that. Susie is your best friend.

    Helpful: Something she did made you angry!

2 "How come my sister gets so many birthday presents?"

    Unhelpful: Well on your birthday you'll get presents and your sister won't.

    Helpful: It can be hard to watch your sister get all those presents. It could make you wish today were your birthday

3 "This picture I made is ugly."

    Unhelpful: No it isn't. It's beautiful.

    Helpful: I can see you're not at all satisfied with the way your picture turned out.

4 "My teacher gives us too many tests."

Unhelpful:	You complain about everything.
Helpful:	If it were up to you, there would be far fewer tests.

5 A child looks unhappy.

Unhelpful:	What's wrong? If you don't tell me what's wrong, I can't help you.
Helpful:	Something is wrong. Something is making you sad.

ABOUT ENGAGING
cooperation

*"It makes me angry when
I tell the kids to do
something and they ignore
me."*

ABOUT ENGAGING COOPERATION

Children find it hard to cooperate when parents blame, call names, threaten, or give orders.

SOME HELPFUL WAYS TO ENGAGE A CHILD'S COOPERATION

PRACTICE

engaging cooperation

In each of the following situations, choose the response most likely to invite cooperation and maintain the child's self-esteem.

1 A child is painting in the living room.

    Parent: **a** If I catch you with those paints in the living room once more, I'll take them away.

            b Paint can stain the carpet. You can paint in the kitchen or in your room. You decide.

            c What is wrong with you? Do you know how hard it is to get paint out of a rug?

2   **Child:** (whining) Mom, you've got to take me for school supplies today! You said you would.

    Parent: **a** Stop that whining!

            b Don't bother me now. Maybe later.

            c Here's how I like to be asked: Mom, could you please take me for school supplies today?

3 A child runs out the door leaving his homework on the table.

    Parent: **a** Jimmy, your homework!

            b Jimmy, come back here. You're such a scatterbrain! Look what you left on the table.

            c You spent the whole night doing your homework and then you go off without it. That's brilliant!

4 Child: Mommy, get off the phone. I have to tell you something.

Parent:
a Leave me alone! Can't I have one conversation in peace?

b Shhh, be quiet! I'll be off soon.

c I'd like to finish talking. You can write what you want to tell me or you can draw it.

5 Your child has neglected to water the plant you bought for her.

Parent:
a You begged me for that plant and now you're letting it die.

b The leaves on your new plant are drooping.

c The next plant I buy you is going to be plastic.

Answers: 1b, 2c, 3a, 4c, 5b

PRACTICE

engaging cooperation

Part II

Your child brushes her teeth and leaves the water dripping in the bathroom sink.

1 What might you say that would not be helpful to his or her self-esteem or to the relationship between you?

_____

_____

_____

2 Show how you might use each of the methods listed below to engage your child's cooperation.

  a Describe what you see.

_____

_____

_____

  b Give information.

_____

_____

_____

c Offer a choice.

_____

_____

_____

d Say it with a word.

_____

_____

_____

e Describe what you feel.

_____

_____

_____

f Write a note.

_____

_____

_____

≡ POSSIBLE ANSWERS ≡

Here are some unhelpful responses to the child who has left the water dripping in the bathroom sink.

Unhelpful: Who left the water running?

How many times do I have to remind you to shut the faucet?

Why are you so careless?

It's because of people like you that we have a water shortage.

Here are some responses that might engage the child's cooperation and leave both parent and child feeling good about themselves and each other.

a <u>Describe what you see.</u>
The water is dripping.

b <u>Give information.</u>
Even a slow drip can waste gallons of water each day.

c <u>Offer a choice.</u>
You can shut the faucet with your right hand or your left hand.

d <u>Say it with a word.</u>
The faucet.

e <u>Describe what you feel.</u>
It bothers me to see precious water being wasted.

f <u>Write a note.</u>
If you hear a drip, drip, drip,
To the sink *quick* make a trip,
Don't let the water get away,
Save it for another day.

Thank you,

The Management

(Kids love rhymes, but a simple "Please shut faucet after use" or HELP END DRIPS can also be effective.)

AN ALTERNATIVE
to punishment

*"When a child does
something really wrong,
shouldn't he be punished?
How else will he learn?"*

THE PROBLEM WITH PUNISHMENT

Many parents believe that the way to discipline a child who has misbehaved is to punish him. These parents are convinced that that's the only way a child will "learn a lesson."

But Most Children Don't React That Way to Being Punished

Some children think . . .

Other children think . . .

Others think . . .

PROBLEM SOLVING

How can parents motivate their children to behave responsibly? Are there alternatives to punishment? One alternative is to sit down with a child and work at solving the problem together. Here's how the problem-solving method works:

Step I. Listen to and acknowledge your child's feelings and needs.

Don't criticize what he says. Encourage him to explore all his feelings.

Sum up your child's point of view.

Step II. Talk about your feelings or needs. (It's best to keep this part short.)

Step III. Invite the child to join you in a search for solutions.

Step IV. Write down all ideas. Don't comment on whether they're good or bad. (If possible let the child go first.)

The teacher is mean. Change my class.

Change class.. Anything else?

Maybe I could change my seat.

Change seat.. What else?

Ask her to call on me. She hardly ever calls on me.

Wants to be called on more often. I wonder why she doesn't.

She says she has to give the other children a chance. But I want her to know I know the answers.

Maybe you could write your answers and show them to her at the end of the period.

Good. And put down that she should call on me at least one time.

Step V. Decide which ideas you don't like, which you do, and how you plan to follow through.

PRACTICE WITH PROBLEM SOLVING

≡   ≡

Imagine that you have a six-year-old daughter, Amy, who is too rough with your eighteen-month-old son, Billy. You've warned Amy over and over again *not* to hurt her brother, but she just ignores you. It's true, sometimes Billy grabs her toys, but you've explained to Amy that her brother is only a baby and doesn't understand. Today Billy tore a page of her favorite book and Amy pushed him so hard that he fell and got a bump on the back of his head. There seems nothing left to do but punish her. But how? You could hit her the way she hits her brother. Or you could forbid her to play with her friends for a week. Or you could take away her new toy.

Instead you decide to listen respectfully to her point of view, share your point of view, and ask her to join you in trying to solve the problem together.

Step I. <u>Listen to and acknowledge your child's feelings or needs.</u> (For example, here's what you might say to bring up the subject:)

> Parent: **I notice that when Billy grabs your toys, you either hit him or push him, because he makes you so angry. Have I got that right?**
> (And here's how your child might respond.)

> Child: **Yeah, he's such a pest. He bothers me all the time. He tore my best book. I *had* to push him. He should play with his own baby toys.**

Parent: (Continue the conversation by acknowledging your child's feelings.) _____ ____

_____

_____

_____

_____

Parent: (Find out if there's anything else her
brother does that bothers her.) _____

_____

_____

_____

_____

Child: (What might she add?) _____

_____

_____

_____

_____

Parent: (Sum up your child's point of view.) _____

_____

_____

_____

_____

Step II. <u>Talk about your feelings or needs.</u>

      Parent: _____

             _____

             _____

             _____

             _____

Step III. <u>Invite the child to join you in a search for solutions.</u>

      Parent: _____

             _____

             _____

             _____

             _____

Step IV. <u>Write down all ideas. Don't comment on whether they are good or bad. If possible, let the child go first.</u> (For example)

send him to live with Grandma

_____

_____

_____

_____

Step V. Discuss which ideas you don't like, which you do, and how you plan to follow through.

Parent: _____

_____

_____

_____

Child: _____

_____

_____

_____

Parent: _____

_____

_____

_____

Child: _____

_____

_____

_____

Step VI. Shake hands on your agreement.

SOLVING THE
PROBLEM TOGETHER

Here's our version of the kind of problem-solving discussion that might take place between a parent and a child who is hitting a younger sibling.

Step I. <u>Listen to and acknowledge your child's feelings and needs.</u>

Parent: I notice that when Billy grabs your toys, you either hit him or push him because he makes you so angry. Have I got that right?

Child: Yeah, he's such a pest. He bothers me all the time. He tore my best book. I had to push him. He should play with his own toys.

Parent: (acknowledging the child's feelings) So when you hit him, it's your way of saying, "Don't break or tear my things. Play with your own toys and leave me alone."

Child: Yeah.

Parent: (finding out if there's anything else the child wants to tell) Is there anything else Billy does that bothers you? I'd really like to know.

Child: The time I let him play with my puzzle, he lost two pieces. And he threw my teddy bear in the toilet.

Parent: (summing up child's point of view) So not only does he bother you when you're playing, but when you try to be nice to him, he either loses your toys or ruins them.

Step II. <u>The parent talks about his or her feelings and</u>
<u>needs.</u>

> **Parent:** Here's how it is from my point of view. I
> get very upset when one of my children
> hurts another of my children.

Step III. <u>The parent invites the child to help in a search for</u>
<u>solutions.</u>

> **Parent:** Let's put our heads together and see if we
> can think of some ways for you to play
> peacefully, keep your toys safe, and at the
> same time make sure your brother doesn't
> get hurt.

Step IV. <u>The parent writes down all ideas without comment-</u>
<u>ing on whether they are good or bad. (She lets the</u>
<u>child go first.)</u>

Child: Send him to live with Grandma.

Parent: I'll write that down. What else?

Child: Make him stay in his crib.

Parent: (writing) Stay in his crib. Okay, anything else?

Child: I could close my door.

Parent: (writing) Close door. We could put the toys you don't want him to touch on a high shelf that he can't reach.

Child: Or put them in my closet.

Parent: I've got that. But what can you do when he takes a book that's special to you?

Child: I could tell him, "That's my book," and give him another one that I don't mind him touching.

Parent: (still writing) And if you want to play by yourself, you can tell him, "I want to play by myself now."

Step V. <u>Parent and child discuss which ideas they don't like,</u>
<u>which they do, and how they plan to follow through.</u>

Parent: Well, I couldn't go along with this first idea of sending him to Grandma. I could never send either of my children away. So we'd better cross that out.

Child: And if we make him stay in his crib, he'll just cry. So cross that out too.

Parent: But you could close your door if you want to be private.

Child: And we could hide my best toys in the closet.

Parent: Do you think you could restrain him gently if he tries to grab a toy you don't want him to touch?

Child: Yeah, but what if I tell him I want to play by myself and he doesn't listen?

Parent: If you try everything we've talked about and it still doesn't work, you can always call me and I'll take him out of your room. But I have the feeling you'll get better and better at figuring out ways to handle Billy gently by yourself.

Step VI. <u>Parent and child shake hands on their agreement.</u>

Parent: Let's shake on the ideas we agreed to and put them up on the refrigerator door to help us both remember.

WHAT IF THE SOLUTION DOESN'T WORK?

Sometimes parents ask, "What if the plan you and your child agree upon works for a while and then fails? Suppose the child reverts to her old ways? What then?"

These are the times that test our determination. We can either go back to lecturing and punishing or we can go back to the drawing board. For example:

Parent: I'm disappointed that our ideas aren't working anymore. I see you've started to hit Billy again and that's not acceptable. Shall we give the old plan another chance? Shall we talk about what's getting in the way? Or do we need to come up with some new ideas?

As parents we realize that even the most perfect plan will not be permanent. What worked for the child when she was six may not work for her when she turns seven. Life is a continual process of adjustment and readjustment—of having to cope with new problems. By involving our children in the search for solutions, we are giving them the tools to help them solve the problems that confront them now—while they're at home—and in the difficult, complex world that awaits them.

PART
II

QUESTIONS
and answers

PARENTS ASK . . .

Whenever we give a program on communication skills to parents, we stop at one point and invite the audience to tell us what's on their minds. After a second of silence, hands fly up everywhere. The sheer number of comments, questions, and urgent concerns remind us how overwhelming the challenges of child rearing can be, and how despite all the ground we've already covered in our talk, there's always more—much more—yet to be explored. On the chance that some of the concerns expressed by our audiences are your concerns as well, we'd like to share with you the questions we're most often asked, along with our answers.

My daughter has been doing a lot of whining lately and it's driving me crazy. How can I stop it?

Before you try to stop the whining, you might want to think about what could be causing it. Is the whining a symptom of tiredness... hunger... jealousy... frustration... anger? Once you've zeroed in on the cause, you can deal with the feeling by respectfully acknowledging it: "I can hear how disappointed you are that I'm not buying you new skates today. Let me write it down on your wish list."

Sounds easy, doesn't it? It isn't. The sound of a whining child can be torture to listen to and can drive the most patient of parents to lash out at the youngster with, "Stop it!" "Why can't you talk like a normal person? You are such a whiner."

But by labeling the child a whiner, we reinforce her whining behavior. Instead we want to encourage our children to get their needs met in more direct and positive ways. For example, if your daughter persists in whining, you can tell her: "Lisa, it's hard for me to listen to you ask for things when you have that sound in your voice. Could you ask me again, using your pleasant voice? That way it will be easier for me to hear you and consider what you want."

My son has a tantrum over the least little thing. For example, when it's time to leave the playground, I usually have to carry him out kicking and screaming. How do I keep him from having these tantrums?

A tantrum is a child's response to powerful emotions that temporarily overwhelm him. When your son was forced to leave an activity he loved, he protested this "injustice" with his whole being, by kicking, screaming and crying. There are two ways you can help him to keep his emotions from boiling over:

1. Let him have plenty of advance notice of your intentions. This gives him a chance to adjust to the idea of having to make the transition from playing to leaving. For example, "Jimmy, we'll be leaving in ten minutes." And again, five minutes later: "You're having such a good time going down the slide. We have to leave for home in five minutes. Do you want to take one more turn on the slide or two more?"

2. You can also give your son in fantasy what you can't give him in reality: "Jimmy, I can see that if it were up to you, you would take ten more turns on the slide. Maybe even a hundred. Boy, do you wish we didn't have to go home now!"

By expressing his wishes in fantasy you make it easier for your son to deal with reality.

* * *

One woman told us that she had recently adopted a four-year-old girl named Emily who had constant tantrums, sometimes lasting more than an hour. It seems that Emily's natural mother had died six months before and since then she had had inconsistent care. The adoptive mother said,

> I've been trying to express what I thought Emily was feeling as she was tantruming, but mostly I tried showing her I understood her feelings *before* the tantrum. "Oh, Emily, that could be frustrating!" or "You must be so upset!" It was as if she never heard me. But last week a miracle happened. We had the perfect setup for a major explosion. Emily had been invited to play with a little girl she had

just met in her nursery school but my sister (she drove her) couldn't find the child's house, gave up, and brought Emily home. I took one look at her face (heavy storm clouds) and said, "You must be so disappointed. You were looking forward to going to Sara's house all day today."

Emily nodded and said, "I'm very sad. Can we go to the park?"

I was amazed at her response and felt terrible to have to disappoint her again. I thought, "This next refusal will really push her over the edge." I kneeled down, put my arm around her and said, "Emily, I wish with all my heart that I could take you, but I can't because I have to go to the dentist."

Her lower lip started quivering. I thought, "Oh no! Here it comes." But it never did. Emily took a deep breath and said, "Can I come with you?"

I said, "Definitely yes, and tomorrow I'm getting directions and taking you to Sara's house myself."

Emily broke into a big smile.

That night I told my husband how relieved and happy I was that Emily didn't scream and cry. My husband said, "Maybe she's growing up."

"Yeah, and maybe I'm helping her," I thought to myself.

I saw my son break a vase in the living room and he denied doing it. What's the best way to handle lying?

A lie usually represents a wish or a fear. Your son wished he hadn't broken your vase and feared your reaction. It's a good idea to deal with the wish or deal with the fear rather than focus on the lying. Notice the difference between these two scenarios:

Mother: Who broke this vase? . . . Did you do it?

Child: Not me.

Mother: Are you sure? Don't lie to me now.

Child: No, I swear I didn't.

Mother: You're a little liar. I saw you do it and now you're going to be punished.

Instead of trying to trap the child in a lie, it would be best to confront the youngster with the truth:

Mother: I saw you throw the ball and break the vase.

Child: No I didn't! I swear.

Mother: I'm sure you wish it hadn't happened. Danny, I'm upset. I expect you to be able to say "no" to yourself when you're tempted to play with a ball in the living room. Now how do we get this mess cleaned up?

Child: I'll get a broom.

By not labeling a child "liar," by accepting his feelings, and sharing our own, we make it safe for him to come to us with the truth.

What do you do about a child who refuses to sit still in a car? How do I *make* him behave?

Whenever you ask yourself, "How do I *make* this child do something," tell yourself you're heading in the wrong direction. A more helpful question would be, "How do I encourage my child to become an active participant in solving the problem?"

One father told us that he had been enraged by his son's "hyper" behavior in the car, despite repeated warnings to the boy to sit still. By the time they got home, the father was furious and ready to punish his son either by taking away his allowance, his TV privileges, or both. Instead he decided to involve his son in finding a solution. He said,

> Michael, I didn't like what happened in the car today. When you jumped up and down in the back seat, your head blocked the window and I almost didn't see that big truck coming up behind us. That was dangerous. For this family's safety I need you to think of three things you could do in the car that would help you to sit quietly.

To his father's surprise, Michael said he wanted to think of *ten* things. The father wrote down all of Michael's ideas and then posted his list on the dashboard of the car. Here's the list Michael came up with:

1. Look at cars and trucks

2. Sing songs—softly

3. Play games with Daddy like "ABC game" (find alphabet letters on signs along the road)

4. Think

5. Chew gum or eat grapes

6. Count all the things in the car

7. Rest

8. Color

9. Watch people through the car windows

10. Read books

The father said that Michael was very pleased with himself, but the best part was seeing his son read his list and use his own ideas.

What can you do about the bickering between the children?

We have written an entire book in answer to this question called *Siblings Without Rivalry*. One of our major recommendations is to involve the children in finding solutions to their problems rather than imposing a solution upon them. A father told us:

My two daughters (five and eight) were fighting over who would sit in the front seat of the car next to Daddy. I said, "Cut it out, girls. Today Annie can sit up front with me and tomorrow Katie can sit there. And if you don't like that idea, here's another: Annie can sit up front on the way to the store and Katie can sit up front on the way home." They didn't like either of my suggestions (which I thought were pretty good) and kept on fighting. Suddenly I remembered to turn it over to them. I said, "Boy, this is a tough problem. But I have a lot of confidence in you two. You'll probably be able to figure out some kind of solution that feels fair to each of you."

They came up with the darndest idea. Since Katie was eight (an even number) and Annie was five (an odd number), they decided to split up the days of the month according to odd and even. On odd days Annie (five) sits in the front. On even days Katie (eight) sits in the front. It's been working beautifully. I don't even have to remind them.

* * *

Even very young children can work out the conflicts between them. One mother wrote to tell us:

I have a success story to report using ideas from your books with a four-year-old and a two-and-a-half-year-old.

My daughter, Shari (two-and-a-half) had invited Molly (four) to spend the afternoon with us. We were all a little cranky, and before long their play in the den became shrill and approached the "pull hair and shove" stage. It seems they both wanted to watch a different video tape.

I was simply too drained to deal with it so I marched in and recited the "routine" like a script: "I can see that you are both really upset. Each of you wants to watch your favorite video, and it's very hard to figure out what to do. You two have been friends for a long time and I'm sure you can settle this in a way that feels good to both of you."

I left the room. Within *one minute* Molly and Shari came into the kitchen HOLDING HANDS! "We decided to watch the end of Molly's video first and then we'll watch the beginning of Shari's video."

I was so proud of them. And proud of myself, too!

How do you feel about giving children "time out"?

Whenever we're uncertain about using a particular method with a child, we ask ourselves, "Is this a method we would like used with ourselves in our most caring relationships?" Suppose, for example, that I had carelessly made out a check on an overdrawn account, causing my husband to receive an embarrassing phone call at work from a bill collector. And further suppose that when he came home from work he said to me sternly, "That's it. I've had it. I am giving you 'time out.' I want you to go into your room right now and think about what you did."

How would I experience his words? I'd feel as if I were being punished or excommunicated. I'd think, "I must be such an awful person that I need to be sent away." Or I might become defiant and counterattack with "I haven't noticed *you* being Mr. Perfect lately. You let the car run out of gas last week," and the fight would be on.

However if *he* took "time out," saying something like "I'm really upset about that bounced check and I don't want to let it out on you. I'm going to sit down with the paper a while and cool off a little," I'd probably feel contrite. Later, I'd tell him how sorry I was to have caused him the embarrassment and tell myself to make sure that it didn't happen again.

We therefore recommend to parents who are thinking of ordering a child to take "time out" that they consider instead taking "time out" for themselves.

One mother told us she said to her two shrieking teenagers, "I am so angry my stomach is churning. I can't listen to this screaming anymore. It's a beautiful day and I'm going out for a walk now." This mother also said she thinks of "time out" as a gift she gives to herself rather than a disciplinary measure to use on her children.

One father informed us that he had progressed from spanking his kids, to using "time-out," to expressing his strong feelings—with few words. He found that one loud, *"I don't like what I see!!"* or "Children, here's what I expect . . ." usually led to improved behavior.

This next question is one that we ask of parents. We know that notes can be a powerful means of communication and so when we give workshops, our question to parents is "How do you use notes?"

Two parents told us that they wrote notes as a way of managing their own angry feelings. Here are their stories.

I have seven children, ages seven to eighteen—four girls and three boys. I get tired of talking and they get tired of listening. So I write them a lot of notes. One day after they left for school I checked their rooms. The girls' room was disgusting—dirty clothes, underwear, food, etc. I was furious. I took my paper and black marker and proceeded to write the girls a letter describing what I saw (a pigsty), what I thought of them (pigs) and what I expected of them when I came home (a clean room or else!). Then I pinned the letter—sheets and sheets of paper on their curtains. As the day passed I would return to the disaster area and reread my letter. Each time I would unpin the pages and rewrite my expectations and feelings on fresh paper in a more civilized form. My final letter was actually friendly. The whole process made me feel better. Putting my frustration in writing gave me a chance to explode and then to choose my words. It gave me time to change from attacking my daughters to attacking the problem.

* * *

This next example is from a single mother.

Situation:

> The living room was a mess—beyond the ability of Jeremy, my six-year-old, to organize the cleanup. It was late, I was tired, and I have a tendency to get very angry when I have to repeat myself and I did not want to supervise *another* cleanup.

My solution:

> On a large piece of paper I listed each task by number and in a new color. I also drew a small picture:

1. Blocks

2. Figures (dolls, robots, puppets)

3. Legos

4. Crayons

5. Books

Jeremy studied my note, smiled, and went to work. Not only did he complete the job, but there were unexpected results:

1. My son's pride at having cleaned up the whole living room by himself.
2. His feeling of self-importance as he crossed off each task ("Mom, one and three are done!")
3. His new image of himself as a "big-guy memo reader."
4. His discovery that a BIG JOB solution is made up of a lot of little jobs.

* * *

It's not likely that you'd ever think of writing a note for a child who is too young to read and yet parents who have tried this approach report success:

My two-year-old kept forgetting to close the potty after using it. His baby brother was old enough to crawl over and splash in it, but not old enough to open the lid. I taped a note to the inside of the potty lid. It said, "Please close lid after using potty."

The older one could not read, but he brought me the note, asked me to read it to him and then taped it back on the lid. He was fascinated that I wrote to him and from then on remembered to close the potty!

I don't like using the television set as a babysitter, but when I'm preparing dinner, I don't want the kids underfoot or fighting with each other. Any suggestions?

One mother we know solved the too-much-TV problem by turning her dinner preparation time into storytime for the whole family. She told her children that she loved to listen to stories while she made dinner and asked them to bring their favorite books to the kitchen to read aloud to her and to each other while she worked. The children loved the idea. They took pride in selecting the stories they would read and listened with great appreciation to each other. The mother reported several other bonuses: The children watched less TV; they became better readers; their vocabulary improved; they fought less with each other. Best of all, the good mood continued into the dinner hour and the stories provided food for family discussion.

Is there any way to help a child cope with her fear of monsters? I've tried telling my daughter that there is no such thing as a monster, but she's still very fearful.

Over the years parents have shared with us a variety of ways to deal with monsters. Some have given their children a magic word to say that would chase the monsters away. Some have taped a note onto the bedroom door: "Monsters Keep Out!" Some buy their children a special stuffed animal, a "brave buddy," who will watch over and protect them through the night. One father concocted a "magic potion" (vinegar and toothpaste) and placed a dish of the strong smelling stuff near the open window to ward off monsters.

In the next few stories you'll read about parents who have encouraged their children to come up with their own solutions. As you read each account you'll notice that the solutions worked primarily because of the parents' acceptance of their children's perceptions and the children's participation in finding their own answers.

My four-year-old, Jesse, had frequent night terrors. He'd scream wildly and it was impossible to calm him. Finally we asked him what he thought he needed to do to make the monsters go away and stay away. Jesse said that maybe a wall could keep the monsters away. My husband asked if we could manage without real wood or stones. Jesse said, "Of course. We'll build an imaginary wall that only monsters can see ... and we'll paint it brown 'cause monsters *hate* brown."

We spent a long time building an imaginary wall around Jesse's bed. After what felt like an hour of piling on mortar and stones Jesse said, "This is great. Now we need some ROAR so when the monsters touch the wall it will ROAR and scare them away."

Jesse ran to the pantry and came back with an empty jar. "What's that for?" we asked.

"There's ROAR in here," he said and then poured the imaginary ROAR on the imaginary wall and kept the jar by his bed so that he could "pour more of it on the spots that were leaking away ROAR."

Jesse chose the solution, participated in the experience and as a result—the monsters moved on.

* * *

At two-and-a-half Michael, under a lot of stress from a new baby, began to have nightmares about terrible monsters living in all of the corners of his room. After a week of trying everything with no success, I asked Michael what he thought I should do. He said, "Sweep them away." I took a broom to the corners of his room, swept the monsters into the hall and out of the door and said, "Good-bye, don't come back!"

After a few days Michael decided that he wanted to confront the monsters. To solve the problem of broom waving by a two-year-old, I suggested the feather duster as the tool of choice. Michael agreed. For about a week he dusted the monsters out of the room, and he's never had a monster in his room since.

* * *

At about age three my son had his first nightmare and for a few nights following he was afraid to go to sleep. I lay down beside him and asked what he thought we could do to make the room feel safe. Much to my surprise he said, "Orange dust will keep it safe."

I said, "Really?"

He said, "Yes and we'll wash out the room with colors." Well I know he loves to paint and draw so I asked, "How do you do that?"

He said, "Close your eyes and feel the blue color wash out your body and swirl out the floor. Then we'll pick up the green and swish it around the roof and corners and swirl it out the floor—down, down, down into the ground." He's never had a nightmare or night fear since.

Can these communication skills be used with older children?

Yes. The principles and skills in *How To Be the Parent You Always Wanted To Be* apply to people of all ages and to all caring relationships. Here are letters from two different mothers who describe touching moments that took place between themselves and their teenagers.

My daughter, Betsy (thirteen), is a hypersensitive, prickly kind of "touch me not" person. It doesn't take much to make her fly off the handle. Yesterday morning I had to get to my "How To Talk . . ." course so I asked my husband to drive Betsy and the younger children to school for me. As I was gathering my things to go, I noticed that Betsy had not allowed enough time to get ready. Her father was fuming as she was fussing with her hair in front of the mirror. "You're going to make me late with all your foolishness," he yelled. "No one is going to care how your hair looks. We've got to go NOW!!"

Betsy looked as if she were going to "lose it." I walked over to her and said, "It's an awful feeling to be rushed— especially when you want to look nice." Well, this child who shuns any physical expression of caring, turned to me, gave me a big bear hug and ran out the door.

* * *

Jaimie, my sixteen-year-old daughter, had a Spanish composition due Monday morning. She had been stewing about it all weekend as she often feels that writing is not

63

her strength. It was Sunday night and I had had a busy day with dinner, chores, paying bills etc. and had settled down in front of the TV to watch a movie. Finally, some rest and relaxation, peace and quiet . . . until Jaimie storms into the room, drops her books on the floor, sighs heavily and begins to write. Out of the corner of my eye I note her agitation.

Jaimie: This is so stupid! The Spanish teacher is such a jerk.

I'm beginning to get annoyed. I'm tempted to say something like, "You knew you had this assignment. Why did you wait 'til the last minute? Stop complaining. You're interfering with my relaxation, etc."

Jaimie would probably have screamed that I didn't understand her or that I never listened. She would have burst out crying, stormed out of the room, angry at me and I would be furious with her.

Luckily the red flag went up in my brain: Teenager in distress!! So instead here's what happened:

Me: Sounds like this assignment is difficult for you.

Jaimie: Yeah (eyes brimming with tears). She's so stupid.

Me: You feel your Spanish teacher was unfair in giving the class this assignment.

Jaimie: No . . . it's just that I thought this class would be more conversational Spanish.

Me: Oh, so you thought you would be speaking, not writing.

Jaimie: (eyes not as teary). Yeah. (She is writing furiously.)

Me: (intermittently). Boy, you're still working hard.

Finally she closed her notebook.

Me: So you've finished. What was your topic?

Jaimie: I had to write about the person I admire most.

Me: Oh, who did you write about?

Jaimie: You.

FOR MORE INFORMATION

If you'd like to learn more ways to communicate helpfully with your children, you can read any or all of the following books by Adele Faber and Elaine Mazlish:

Liberated Parents/Liberated Children: Your Guide to a Happier Family

How To Talk So Kids Will Listen & Listen So Kids Will Talk

Siblings Without Rivalry: How To Help Your Children Live Together So You Can Live Too

Would you like to get together with other parents who want to learn communication skills? For more information about the seven session *How To Talk So Kids Will Listen Group Workshop Kit* (an audio-cassette program) or the six session *"How To Talk . . ."* video series, please send a self-addressed stamped business envelope to:

Faber/Mazlish
P.O. Box 64
Albertson, NY 11507